Black in White

Her locks unveiled

and other poems from the
Black in White Poetry Competition 2023

CHARLOTTE SHYLLON

+ 36 contributing poets

© Charlotte Shyllon, 2023

First published in 2023 by Paragon Publishing, Rothersthorpe

Cover design: Christine Welby www.1stimpression.org

Front cover illustration: Tia Diana Draws IG: @tiadianadraws

Images used under license from Shutterstock.com

www.blackinwhiteservices.co.uk

Transforming Words Ltd. trading as *Black in White*

ISBN 978-1-78792-030-9

Book design, layout and production management by Into Print
www.intoprint.net
+44 (0)1604 832149

CONTENTS

Dedication and Acknowledgements 6

Foreword. 7

Introduction.. 9

SECTION 1: Black in White Poetry Competition 2023 13

- About the poetry competition   15
- Meet the judges   17
- Why we chose our winners   20

SECTION 2: Poems by Charlotte Shyllon 23

- My new poems: Inspiration and context   24
- A seat at the table   27
- I shouldn't have to…   31
- Take a stand   35
- I'm no victim   39
- White tears happen   43

SECTION 3: Guest Poets' Poems 45

- Inclusion: a love note – Rebecca Caine   47
- At work – Rebecca Caine   51
- Unapologetically Black! – Peju Abuchi   55
- "Other" – Serena Malcolm   59
- I am an African American – Zara Koso-Thomas   61

SECTION 4: Winning Poems 2023 – Workplace Category .. 63

- 1st prize: Her locks unveiled – Zab Birch   65
- 2nd prize: Disciplinary action? – Broken Glass   69
- 3rd prize: Monkey climbing a tree – Andrae Davis 73

SECTION 5: Winning Poems 2023 – Childhood Category. .. 75

- 1st prize: Crabs in a crab pot – Linda Downs   77
- 2nd prize: Regrettable – Janice Whyne   81
- 3rd prize: Exploding teddy bears – A J Pettigrew   85

SECTION 6: Highly Commended Poems 2023 (in alphabetical order).. 87

- A broken child – Jacquie Burgwin-Turner [Childhood]   88
- A mother's plea – Sarah Wood [Childhood]   91
- Angry Black woman – Michelle Brooks [Workplace]   93
- Assumptions – Farnaz Rais [Workplace]   95
- Australia fair – Sarah Lock [Workplace]   97
- First day – Olugbemi [Workplace]   99
- Folk tales and fables – Laurie O'Garro [Workplace]   100
- Get back in your cage – Neleh Yartel [Workplace]   103
- How BHM has me feeling – Riley Taylor [Childhood]   105
- Meetings – Farnaz Rais [Workplace]   107
- Mrs Able – Dean Gordon [Childhood]   108
- Never stood a chance (an odyssey) – Juley-Ann Smith [Workplace]   109
- Not/in your favour – A K Castellan [Workplace]   114
- School survivor 1984 – Rabia Begum [Childhood]   116
- Self-racism – Alexandra Thomas [Childhood]   117
- The damage your words do – Leah Hodgson-Clark [Childhood]   119
- The initiation – Simon Smailes [Childhood]   121
- The innocence of a child – Poetry Girl 3.0 [Childhood]   123
- The workplace is full of it – Ruby Joseph [Workplace]   124
- Them and us – Olugbemi [Childhood]   126
- This time it's personal - Sandra Howell [Childhood]   129
- Two strong – Nalo Solo [Childhood]   132
- What are you? – Alisha Fernandes [Workplace]   133
- What have you learnt? Parts 1 and 2 – Annie Alleyne [Childhood]   135
- When you grow up – Emma Evans [Childhood]   137

- Where the monster crumbles – Jonxthon [Workplace] 138
- Where you came from – Zainab Tasneem [Workplace] 139
- Whitewashed – Leah Hodgson-Clark [Childhood] 142
- You're triggered – Sharon Hood [Childhood] 144

SECTION 7: About Black in White. .. .. .147

- About us 149
- Our products 149
- Our services 149
- Sponsorship opportunities 150
- Our team 150
- Contact us 151

Dedication

This book, like its predecessors, is dedicated to all those who see and value the benefits of equity, diversity and inclusion, and who labour actively in whatever capacity within this field to help open the minds of those who are the reason why these poems have been written...

Acknowledgements

I would like to acknowledge several people who have been instrumental in helping me to compile the contents for this book.

- 😊 All the poetry competition entrants, especially those featured in this book. Without their poems, this book wouldn't be as content rich as it is. Not everyone could be selected and celebrated publicly, but I appreciate everyone's efforts.

- 😊 My fellow judges in the Black in White Poetry Competition who diligently undertook an iterative judging process to select the winning and highly commended poems.

- 😊 The members of the Black in White team who give many hours to our common passion project.

- 😊 All my other family and friends who gave an encouraging word or two along the way.

- 😊 My children who share their mother with her laptop on all those mornings, nights and weekends when I work on Black in White activities, and provide support and inspiration.

Most of all, I thank God for giving me the strength and focus to continue on this journey.

FOREWORD

I have always loved reading poetry, so when I was asked to write the foreword for the fourth Black in White anthology, I was humbled, honoured and jumped at the opportunity. I have always found the artistry of conveying a plethora of emotions through the story telling in poetry to be such a great talent. This anthology is filled with enlightening, moving, inspirational and timely poems, focusing on experiences of racism from childhood to the workplace.

Why timely? In the last few years of this current government, there appears to be an acceptance of incendiary language, targeted at 'differences' or 'otherness', with the danger of creating even more of a divided society based on race. This we must address. Words have consequences. You would think that with developments in the 21st century of legislation related to equality and diversity and organisations having equality, diversity and inclusion polices, race would be considered an issue that is important to address. However, the horror of the Child Q case and the disproportionate number of Black women who die in childbirth in the UK are examples that remind us that we cannot be complacent when it comes to racism and that policies are sometimes a tick-box exercise and have no weight to address concerns regarding race.

Reading these poems at times made me tearful and angry, but also strengthens my resolve to know lessons can be learnt from these poems and provide a basis for empowering actions. This amazing compilation of poems resonates in every way with lived experiences for many people of colour. Ordinary people have presented extraordinary stories through the power of poetry, shedding light on the challenges of racism, so we never forget its ugliness and we recognise the need to address it if we as a people are to progress.

The space provided by Charlotte to enable poets to present their stories is phenomenal, as there are limited opportunities for poets reflecting on such an emotive subject of race to be able to publish.

I am reminded of a quote from one of my favourite poems, written by the great Queen Maya Angelou: *'You may kill me with your hatefulness, but still I rise'*.

You will rise, empowered, reading these beautiful poems.

Dr Marvelle Brown
Associate Professor – Programme Team Lead for Public Health
PhD, MPhil, Post-Grad Dip (Ed), SFHEA, Post-Grad Dip (Health & Social Research), Post-Grad Cert LMCC, (BSc (Hons) Social Policy, RN, RM, RHV, RNT
University of Hertfordshire

INTRODUCTION

Penning poems on racism:
Being informed, being inspired, being intentional

Being informed

If anyone had told me three years ago that I would be running a social enterprise alongside my main business to share poems about racism and open minds to equity, diversity and inclusion (EDI) principles, I wouldn't have believed it. But here we are.

For most of my working life I didn't speak about racism. I relied on my education and class to open doors for me, as they had while I was growing up as a privileged diplomat's daughter. I'd never had to 'play the race card', so at work I pretended I didn't see the microaggressions, slights and sometimes intentional put downs. I told myself that it was just because I had messed up or wasn't good enough, or because I am a woman, or because of personal challenges I was dealing with, or whatever. So I developed coping strategies, pushed through the fear and outwardly appeared to thrive.

When George Floyd was murdered, everything changed and my journey to founding Black in White commenced. Via Black in White, I can be vocal and give others an opportunity to have their voices heard too. Today we run annual poetry competitions to elicit poems about racism in the workplace and in childhood. We have four anthologies in our portfolio to date, including this one, plus a product range comprising discussion guides, posters and postcards. We provide EDI consultancy services and participate in a variety of events and meetings to share our experiences of racism through poetry. We are making an impact, albeit a modest one at present; and I believe we can do so much more.

Alongside sharing lived experiences, I am on a journey to becoming more informed about race issues in the wider EDI context. Being informed on race is important for us all. I educate myself by following people in this area with more knowledge and expertise than I have. I am also part-way through a Master's level qualification on 'Strategic approaches to equality, diversity and inclusion' which I plan to conclude this year.

With increasing learned expertise in this area, I have been able to expand the range of poems that I create. Most of my earlier poems were about things that have happened to me personally or that I have been told about. Alongside this, I now also write poems about broader race-related topics, including diversity fatigue (in the third Black in White anthology — recently retitled as *Here is Your Heart*) and white tears (in this book).

Being inspired

While Black in White has allowed me to be vocal about racism, being vocal comes at a cost. Speaking about race and racism makes a lot of people feel uncomfortable. Period. Even some working in the EDI space have expressed discomfort with the level of prominence being given to race versus some other protected characteristics. I cover this in a new poem **A seat at the table.**

Speaking about race can also make you, the person vocalising the issues, uncomfortable. Logically, I know this — yet I wasn't really prepared for it when I started Black in White, and it took me a while to understand what was happening. Many people contributing in this space experienced this long before I did. In her book, *Why I'm No Longer Talking to White People About Race* (Bloomsbury Publishing, 2017), author Reni Eddo-Lodge shares some insights on this. She describes talking about race as 'emotionally exhausting' and says: "The options are: speak your truth and face the reprisal, or bite your tongue and get ahead in life."

Many Black people who make it into mid- to senior echelons of industry choose to bite their tongue. I get it; that's what I did for nearly three decades. When you start speaking out about racist incidents, some people think you're doing it because you feel victimised while others think you're foolish for not biting your tongue. I talk about this in a new poem **I'm no victim.**

Even though I consider myself a winner, not a victim, I have wrestled at times with what the potential impacts of speaking out might be. Will it affect my main business? Am I now considered an activist? How do I feel about that? These questions and more come to my mind from time to time. However, now that I have woken up to the issues surrounding race, I can't 'unknow' what I know. And knowing what I know, I can't back down. So I continue.

I have learned that in order to keep active in this area, I need to keep myself inspired. I am inspired by many people operating in the field who are so much more vocal than I am, and clearly face any reprisals head on. People like Dr Shola Mos-Shogbamimu, Professor Kehinde Andrews, Professor John Amaechi, OBE, Shereen Daniels, and more. Hats off to them all. They have a platform and are not afraid to speak their truth.

I am inspired by those long gone who were unafraid to speak out boldly, notably of course Martin Luther King, Malcom X and Maya Angelou. Recently, I watched a video of Mohammed Ali being interviewed in Ireland in 1972. The interviewer asked him if he believed all white people are devils. In his response, Ali drew a powerful analogy; he said if you are in an environment with 10,000 rattlesnakes and you know that 1,000 of them don't want to bite you, because there is no way of identifying the 'good' snakes, you have to protect yourself against the 9,000 bad snakes. So you shut your door.

I am inspired every year by those who enter our poetry competition, sharing their experiences of and perspectives on racism. Running this competition is one of the most rewarding elements of the work we do at Black in White. That's why it's become an annual fixture on our calendar, and we hope to continue to build on it, encouraging more people to enter and trying to reach more people through the resulting anthologies.

Being intentional

In my daily life I am now more intentional about anti-racism, calling out racial discrimination or prejudice where I observe it or suspect this is at the root of certain behaviours I encounter. It doesn't always go down well. Earlier this year, I wrote an article about the racist treatment of people of Black African origin by airport police in Casablanca airport, Morocco, as I travelled through there, and how they mistreated me because I recorded their actions on my mobile phone.

But being intentionally anti-racist is a must. As Dr Beverly Daniel

Tatum, a psychologist and author of *Can We Talk About Race?* (2007), told CNN: "Unless I'm really being intentional and thinking about how to interrupt the racist policies and practices that are surrounding me, then my silence is supporting that."

At Black in White we continue to be intentionally anti-racist by sharing poems and opening minds. As a social enterprise, we rely on volunteers to help us. We need people with the right skills to help promote the poetry competition. We need people to help open doors for us in the corporate and education sectors. We need sponsorship to help us cover the costs of the poetry competition and the prizes, so we can expand the categories. For example, I'd love to introduce a separate category for under-18s, with its own prizes.

If anything you already know about Black in White or have read about in this introduction resonates with you and you would like to join our team, please reach out to me to initiate a conversation about how you could help. My email address is: charlotte@blackinwhiteservices.co.uk.

The journey continues…

Charlotte Shyllon,
Founder and Chief Creative Officer, Black in White

SECTION 1:

Black in White
Poetry Competition 2023

Black in White
Poetry Competition
2023

Have you experienced racism, prejudice, unconscious bias or microaggressions as a child or as a working adult?

Write about your experiences in a poem and enter this year's Poetry Competition. Your poem could help bring insight and illumination to the race-related issues that many people of colour experience, to build understanding and drive change.

This year's categories:
1. Workplace racism · 2. Childhood racism

You could win one of our top cash prizes per category:

1st prize £250

2nd prize £125

3rd prize £75

The winning poems and around 25 highly commended entries will be published in a new Black in White book, to be launched in October during Black History Month, and the contributors will receive a complimentary copy.

To enter:
1. Log onto www.blackinwhiteservices.co.uk/store, pay £1.50 per poem and obtain a payment reference*
2. Send your entry as a Word attachment by email to competition@blackinwhiteservices.co.uk, quoting your payment reference

Don't delay, get writing today!

* Under 18 enter free. Poems must be your own work, previously unpublished, any style and any length. You can submit as many poems as you want. Poems are judged anonymously, so please do not include your name on the attachments. Full competition rules available at www.blackinwhiteservices.co.uk/poetry-competition-about-rules. For further information contact: info@blackinwhiteservices.co.uk.

Closing date: Friday 14th July

Black in White
www.blackinwhiteservices.co.uk

About the Poetry Competition

How it got started

After the release of my first book of poems *Black in White* in November 2020, I decided to run a poetry competition to give other people an opportunity to air some of their experiences of racism in their own voices. The first Black in White Poetry Competition was open for entries during Summer 2021. The judging panel selected three winners and 25 highly commended entries. We announced the results in September and two months later launched an anthology titled *Black in White Community Collection* (since retitled *Foreign Body*). This comprised the 28 selected entries as well as poems written by five guest poets and me.

We ran a bigger and better poetry competition in 2022 extending the entry categories to two, calling for experiences of racism in the workplace and in childhood. The judging panel selected the winners and highly commended entries and the resulting anthology *Black in White Community Collection Volume 2* (retitled *Here is Your Heart*) was launched during the UK's Black History Month celebration in October.

This year's poetry competition, the third, again has been raised to a new level. We have retained the two categories and now award separate prizes for both. The name of this anthology, *Her Locks Unveiled*, is the title of the winning poem in the workplace category. The new naming convention has been designed to ensure each anthology has a distinct identity.

The poetry competition is now an annual fixture on the Black in White calendar, so look out for the launch announcements on 21 March, which is World Poetry Day and International Day for the Elimination of Racial Discrimination.

The judging process

Every year we follow a rigorous judging process. We convene a judging panel, this year one per category, to review and score the poems. We bring new judges on board every year, including some of the prize winners from our previous poetry competitions. The mix of perspectives makes for a well-rounded and inclusive approach.

The judges review all the entries anonymously. We receive entries from the UK, and from other countries including the USA, Germany, Australia and India. Judging involves a detailed initial sift and first round scoring of the poems by each of the judges individually against six criteria: 1) beauty, power, education or entertainment; 2) technical excellence; 3) form and flow; 4) choice of words and readability; 5) polish and expertise; and 6) overall impact.

The scores are summarised and the poems listed in order based on the total scores they receive. The judges then review and discuss this allocation to ensure that the winning and highly commended selections exemplify the competition's objectives.

This year, we awarded six main prizes to the 1st, 2nd and 3rd placed winners in both categories. We awarded 28 poems as highly commended. As in previous years, we received multiple entries from several entrants; because poems are reviewed anonymously, three poets have two poems each in this book.

Meet the Judges

Seven amazing judges joined me in reviewing, scoring and selecting our winning and highly commended poems this year. Read about them below:

Workplace category

Peju Abuchi is a Spoken Word Artist, a potent combination of passion, poetry and pizzazz. Her superpower is her ability to fuse the art of diplomacy and the heart of poetry to educate, elevate and empower minds at every level of society. She has been featured on BBC Radio, Channels TV, The Mayor's Office and Black Inclusion Week.

Rebecca Caine, winner of last year's Black in White poetry competition, has had poems published in Words of Wandsworth, Spectrum magazine and various online poetry blogs and websites. New to writing poetry, she is loving learning to use it as an outlet for her emotional life experiences. She is currently working on her first collection of poetry.

Marcia McKnight has had a 30-year public relations and marketing communications career in the NHS, local government and charity sectors. Marcia was the first black director of communications in a NHS Trust. She is a qualified nurse, former chair of school governors and victim support volunteer. She is also a member of the Black in White team.

Childhood category

Aretha Ahunanya is a 21-year-old student with a deep love for the arts. Having won Beyond the Box's Poetry Competition in 2020, she was later commissioned to write a poem for Open City's 2021 Manifesto: 'Architecture for a New Generation'. Last year, Black in White awarded Aretha 2nd prize for her piece 'Monotypic Blackness'. She is studying Engineering & Architecture at university, and aims to promote diversity within the industry.

Serena Malcolm is an ex-police officer who has been writing poetry for over three decades. She draws influence from her time in the force, her work in youth and mental health services, and her experiences as a woman of mixed heritage growing up in London. She currently works for a local authority. Her poem 'Foreign Body' won 1st prize in the 2021 Black in White Poetry Competition.

Tia Miles is a spoken word poet from East London. As well as writing poetry, she loves performing at open mics across London. Creativity is important to Tia, and she always encourages everyone to express themselves as often as they can, through poetry or other creative means. Tia is the illustrator who creates the beautiful illustrations on the front covers of the Black in White books.

Sarah Murray is a social worker, a keen advocate for social justice. She is passionate about young people reaching their full potential, through education, encouragement, and creativity. She exhibits a 'can do attitude' and is a natural at networking. Sarah is also a member of the Black in White team.

Why We Chose Our Winners

The poems submitted into the poetry competition this year were incredible. They told tales ranging from frightening to hopeful. A veritable treasure trove of insights, illumination and inspiration!

They were penned by people describing situations that occurred as far back as the 1960s right up to the present day. They were written by those directly involved, those who observed the occurrences, and those commenting on stories that appeared in the media. They included perspectives of people from different races and cultures. They were submitted by children as young as 10 years-old to retired adults.

You may be wondering how we chose our winners in both categories from this rich repository of rhymes. With difficulty! The two final judging sessions lasted 90 minutes each and we made good use of every minute. The highly commended entries were included primarily based on their scores and the judges' comments from the detailed first round review. We then carefully considered and aligned on our choice of the top three poems. We explain why these were selected below.

Workplace category

❖ 1ˢᵗ prize: Her locks unveiled – Zab Birch
❖ 2ⁿᵈ prize: Disciplinary action? – Broken Glass
❖ 3ʳᵈ prize: Monkey climbing a tree – Andrae Davis

Much has been written about race and aesthetics, including Black women's hairstyles which in a workplace context are sometimes considered 'unprofessional'. In **Her locks unveiled**, Zab Birch tells a tale of one Black woman who embraced her natural hair, experienced microaggressions but smartly rose above the biases and built understanding. We chose this as the winner in this category not only because it is a beautifully crafted poem, but because it also perfectly exemplifies the approach we advocate at Black in White. As one judge commented, it "elevates the power of mindset... to break down barriers".

Disciplinary action? by Broken Glass (pen name) is a powerful poem that covers the detrimental systemic impacts that some people may face when they feel safe enough to demonstrate vulnerability in the workplace.

The poem doesn't explicitly mention race, but it was selected as our second prize winner because it is hugely relatable for many people of colour who have had similar questions and confusion about the unexpectedly harsh treatment that has been meted out to them in workplace situations where they had expected understanding and support. Judges' comments included "it really spoke to me" and "a strong poetic story on the organisational impact on our mental health".

Andrae Davis' **Monkey climbing a tree** is about the impact racist abuse and behaviours by some pupils had on a teacher who had been hopeful and positive at the start of his teaching job. Burned by his experiences, he concludes that even if you achieve success in society or at work, some people's perceptions of Black people as monkeys will never change. One judge said that this poem shows the "sad reality of the state of certain young minds" and another felt that the poem was "impactful, powerful and important", creating a strong case to educate all children early on equality.

Childhood category
- ❖ 1ˢᵗ prize: Crabs in a crab pot – Linda Downs
- ❖ 2ⁿᵈ prize: Regrettable – Janice Whyne
- ❖ 3ʳᵈ prize: Exploding teddy bears – A J Pettigrew

Linda Downs' poem, **Crabs in a crab pot**, provides a historical account of racism in a school in the UK in the 1960s. It raises many points succinctly about some issues Black children faced in the playground. One would like to think that things are very different nowadays, but poems about situations today disabuse us of this notion. Some of these issues are still very current. But what the judges really found powerful was how the poem concludes. Two judges described the strength in togetherness and hope that it exemplifies in children at such a tender age as "beautiful".

Regrettable by Janice Whyne is the author's take on the response by the authorities to the Child Q case. She was the school girl who was left traumatised after being strip-searched while on her period at school by police in Hackney, London, due to an unfounded suspicion that she had used drugs. The author examines the use of the term 'regrettable' and how unconscionable it is as a response to acts of racism against Black children.

Judges said this poem was "powerful", and the narrative "clear"and "articulate".

With A J Pettigrew's **Exploding teddy bears** poem, we're back in the school playground with a bang. This, too, speaks of times past using metaphors to great effect to demonstrate how much damage "innocent" words can do. One judge commented: "very powerful use of imagery – the writer weaponises childhood elements in such a unique way: 'razors swaddled in blankets, or plastic explosives swallowed by teddy bears'." A very salient reminder about why we need to teach all children about diversity, equality and inclusion from an early age.

Shout out to everyone

There were some excellent poems that didn't make it into this book purely because that's the nature of competitions. The other judges and I would like to thank everyone for their entries and encourage all of those not included to keep telling your stories. Your voice is valued, respected and important.

SECTION 2:

Poems by Charlotte Shyllon

My New Poems: Inspiration and Context

The inspiration and context for each of the five new poems I have written for this book are described below:

* ❖ **A seat at the table:** While attending an equality, diversity and inclusion Masters level training course I was shocked (perhaps naively?) to hear some professionals working in the field bemoaning the fact that race is currently getting more attention; they felt it was impinging on other protected characteristics. I kept quiet initially, while processing this, but by the third time it was mentioned, I had to comment. Such race-focused diversity fatigue is unwarranted, and that's why I call it out in this poem.

* ❖ **I shouldn't have to…:** I was attending a wedding at a smart hotel in Whitehall, London and arrived slightly early, so went to the bar for a drink. It took a while for any of the waiters to come over and attend to me. Yet as I sat there, I observed them being very attentive whenever a white person came in. I maintained my dignity and simply commented "Oh at last!" with a wry smile when a waiter eventually came over to take my order. As I sat there sipping my drink, I penned this poem.

* ❖ **Take a stand:** I am unapologetically primarily a rhyming poet, but even so I hesitated initially about including this poem in this book! If you are a fan of rhyming poems this one has it in abundance… it uses lots of words that rhyme with 'stand'. If you're not a fan, overlook the overabundance of rhyming and focus on the message. It's a call to action to other Black people in particular, and to all of us generally, to take a stand against racism.

* ❖ **I'm no victim:** I have found that some people think if you share stories about racist incidents you've experienced, it's because you feel like a victim. Yes, racism is an act of victimisation; but you don't have to feel like or act like a victim. This poem explains why, by speaking out against racism, I choose instead to be a winner.

❖ **White tears happen:** Recently, I watched Shereen Daniels (shereen-daniels.com) sharing some insights on white tears on LinkedIn. I also watched the Netflix film on Emmett Till, whose murder in 1955 in America's deep South was as a result of white tears. Then the Lucy Letby case threw up the issue of white tears again; she deployed them and was allowed to carry on killing babies in her care, while the Asian doctor who raised concerns about her was told to apologise. This poem shares these and other examples of white tears to flag this as a real issue, albeit controversial, that should not be allowed to happen.

Charlotte's poems from the four anthologies published to date, including most of the above, are available in Black in White (second edition 2023, £14.99). Some of Charlotte's poems are also available as individual postcards, posters and discussion guides (priced from £3.99 to £7.99 + postage & packaging) from www.blackinwhiteservices.co.uk/store.

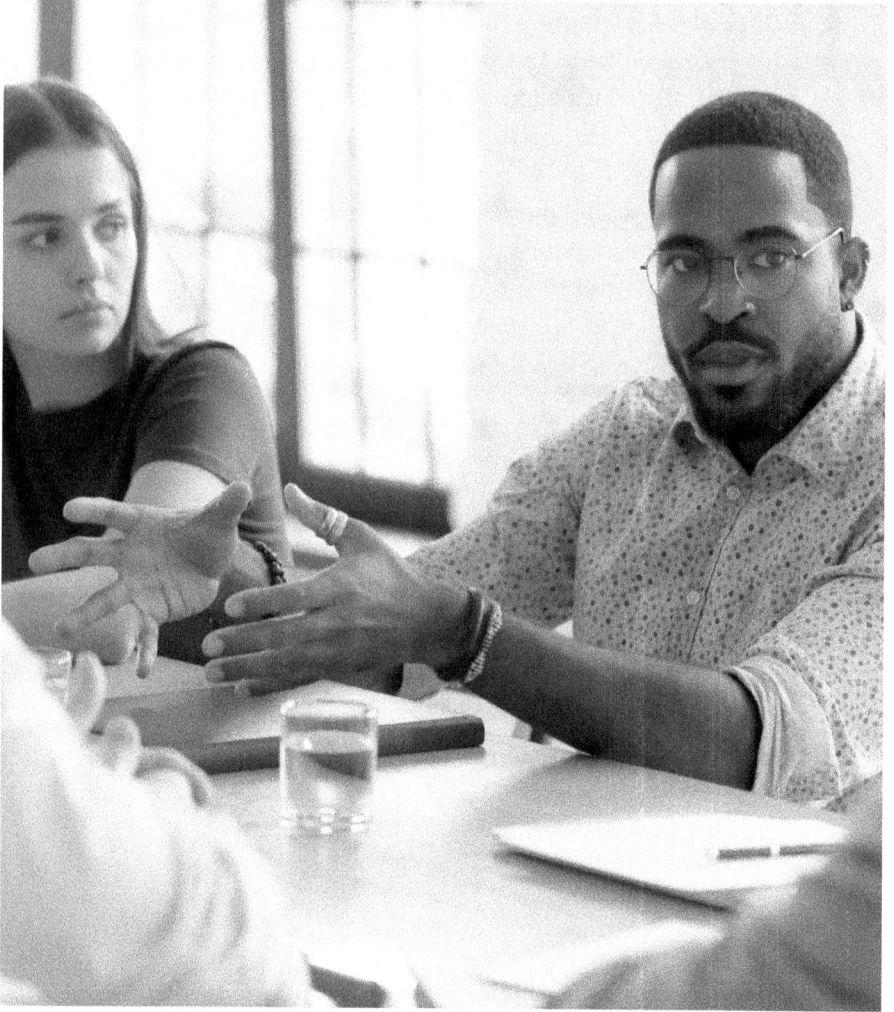

A SEAT AT THE TABLE

By Charlotte Shyllon

Today race is getting more attention,
But this is causing some dissension.
In previous days, race was often ignored,
Now some think we've gone overboard.

Even some working in diversity and inclusion
Seem to have come to this conclusion.
But race deserves its place on the agenda,
With disability, age, sex and gender.

Nine protected areas in the Equalities Act,
Each deserve equality, that's a fact.
Now race is getting its seat at the table,
Give it a chance to become stable.

Race is flavour of the month in October;
We get drunk on it, then must get sober.
When November hits, it's back to reality,
Race dropped again, with force like gravity!

Talking about race shouldn't be for a season,
Or because George Floyd gave us a reason.
Some companies got woke, got in on the act,
Pledged their support, after the fact.

But three years on from George's demise,
If you look around, you could surmise
It's almost back to business as usual;
The priority then has become, well, casual.

It's not enough to look good from the outside,
If your business needs a revamp on the inside.
Superficial change is not enough,
When life for many continues to be tough.

Race issues can be tough, that's for sure.
But talking about it is part of the 'cure'.
Keep race at the table, swallow the bitter pill.
Become anti-racist, it's grist to the mill.

Advocate for all races to be treated the same,
Whatever one's skin colour, nationality or name.
For the sake of those at school, work or rest,
Equality, diversity and inclusion is the best.

Quotable Quotes

"We have no hope of solving our problems without harnessing the diversity, the energy, and the creativity of all our people."

Roger Wilkins

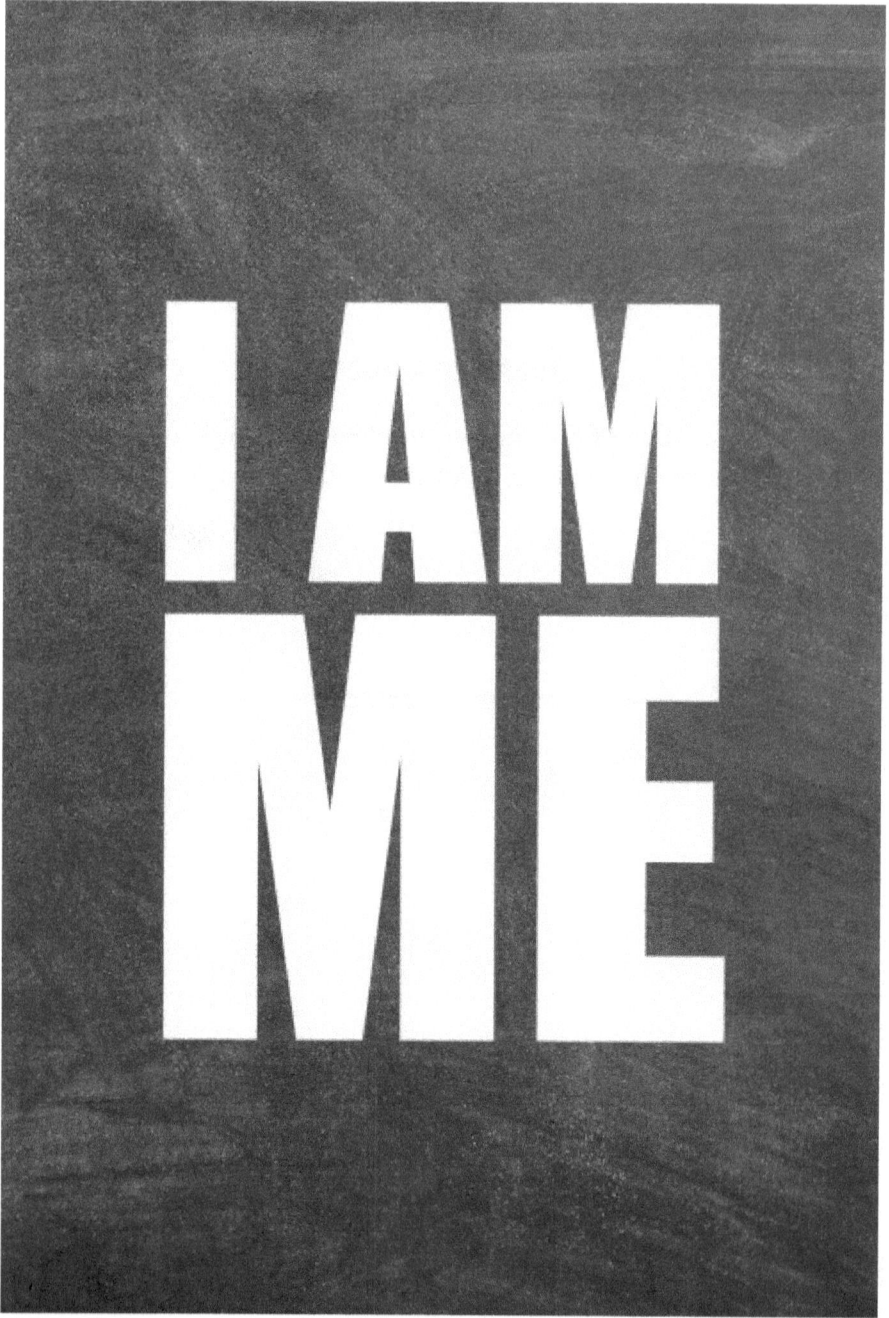

I SHOULDN'T HAVE TO...

By Charlotte Shyllon

I shouldn't have to…
Look a particular way,
Act a particular way,
Sound a particular way,
Dress a particular way,
Be a particular way,
For you to see me.

I shouldn't have to…
Suppress the real me,
Mask the real me,
Adapt the real me,
Refine the real me,
Redefine the real me,
For you to accept me.

I shouldn't have to…
Always try to fit in,
Always start on the back foot,
Always ensure I've not slipped up,
Always be nice even if you're not,
Always have to try harder,
For you to value me.

I shouldn't have to...
Change my name,
Change my hair,
Change my social class,
Change my car,
Change my address,
For you to respect me.

I am me.
See me.
Accept me.
Value me.
Respect me.

I AM ME.

Quotable Quotes

"Prejudice is a burden that confuses the past, threatens the future and renders the present inaccessible."

Maya Angelou

TAKE A STAND

By Charlotte Shyllon

People of our brand,
Black not tanned,
Who work in this land,
Must take a stand.

We can't be bland,
No more head in the sand,
Take courage by the hand,
Be bold, take a stand.

We may need to command,
Or even to grandstand,
Or issue a reprimand.
Whatever. Just take a stand.

Don't be afraid to demand,
If that's the way to disband
Racist thinking, so it's canned.
Always take a stand.

Since we've seen it at first-hand,
We should help all understand
That racism should be banned.
That's why we take a stand.

Whether this is our birthland,
Or we're from a different homeland,
We may find ourselves in wasteland,
Unless we take a stand.

We may never have the upper hand
Unless we learn to withstand,
Learn to avoid the quicksand,
Learn to take a stand.

We need allies to join our band
To correct those who act underhand,
Those who choose to misunderstand,
Because we take a stand.

Closed mindsets need to expand,
To stretch like a rubber band,
Then, when we reach the promised land,
We won't need to take a stand.

Quotable Quotes

"Diversity is a mix and inclusion is making the mix work."

Andrés Tapia

I'M NO VICTIM

By Charlotte Shyllon

Don't call me a victim
Because I refuse to stay schtum;
A victim is a person who hasn't recovered,
Whose struggles are sometimes undiscovered,
Who hasn't overcome the abuse they faced,
Whose true potential someone erased.

I choose to talk about racism,
Even if it's not a popular ism.
Speaking out takes courage,
I seek to encourage, not disparage.
Some applaud, empathise, thank me.
Others say, 'Just let it be'.

So in the quest to tackle racism
I ignore criticism, embrace optimism.
Even if the response I sometimes provoke
Isn't what I want to evoke,
I simply choose to reject
Any kind of disrespect.

Yet what I find really uncool,
Are those who think I'm just a fool.
A fool for speaking out my truth

About things that happened in my youth.
A fool for stopping the pretence,
To some it simply makes no sense.

By exposing racism I'm no fool or sinner,
I'm nobody's victim, I choose to be a winner.
Despite racists met and those still ahead,
I continue to rise, to get out of bed.
I choose to survive, to thrive, to energise,
So don't feel that I need you to apologise.

Apology accepted. But action is better
Against belittlers who continue to fetter.
The fact is our work isn't done,
Call out racism until it's gone.

Though it can be tough, testing, thankless, demanding,
With time and tolerance, we can build understanding.

Quotable Quotes

"Before God, we are all equally wise, and equally foolish."

Albert Einstein

WHITE TEARS HAPPEN

By Charlotte Shyllon

I happened to think of this expression
during an insightful LinkedIn post.
The video showed a discussion
with speakers and an expert host.
When a white woman turns on the tears
a person of colour disappears.
White tears.

It happened to young Emmett Till;
he whistled at a white woman, and she cried.
He was abducted, tortured, killed
but his white murderers cleared, when tried.
Today, lynching has been banned
but the intentions remain underhand.
White tears.

It happened to a doctor, an Asian man,
who complained about a white nurse.
He wanted her checked out, issued with a ban;
but though babies had died, they called him perverse.
Told to apologise, he got a grilling
and she was allowed to carry on killing.
White tears.

It happened to an executive, a Black female boss,
whose white female colleague had failed to impress.
With clients unhappy, she was at a loss,
so called her boss racist, to distract from her mess.
Her complaint was baseless, she had nothing to say,
but tried to discredit her boss anyway.
White tears.

It happened to a Black girl whose two white friends
colluded to exclude her from holiday plans.
She learned of it by chance, it changed her lens
when she saw her friends sporting their tans.
She kept her cool, but told them she was hurt,
they cried as if she had dished the dirt.
White tears.

It happened to me when, apparently, one day
I 'made' a senior white colleague cry.
Really it was just a power play;
I hadn't seen her cry, couldn't understand why.
Though I faced rejection, I refused to say sorry,
and now with insight I can tell this story.
White tears.

They happen. Like white privilege realised,
like white supremacy by another name.
'Dangerous and insidious', they are 'weaponised',
'to invoke sympathy, to divert blame'.
The reality for Black people is no lie
white tears can end up making *them* cry.
Black tears.

* *Quotes from 'White Tears/Brown Scars' by Ruby Hamad, Published by Hachette UK, 2020.*

SECTION 3:

Guest Poets' Poems

INCLUSION: A LOVE NOTE

By Rebecca Caine

I wanted to write a love note
to all who have gone before
Paving the way
from shore to shore

Mary Seacole, Walter Tull
Bernie Grant, Edward Enninful,
Important names you'll hear
in your black history month

But for all the great black Britons
the UK still struggles to include
For every champion who overcame
there are countless others to elude

We look to past heroes
but it's all who chore
So I'd like to give thanks
to those who helped me find my more:

Christopher, the only black child at my school
this first must have been so hard for you

My Dad, singing me 'young gifted and black' from the womb
the message seeped in and gave me strength

Uncle Clinton, cooking callaloo while singing Day-O,
a traditional folk song from where I was from

Cousin Karen, for gently platting my hair
showing me what black beauty was about

My Grandma, for her black eyes and soft gaze
it was true love looking right back

Change doesn't happen overnight
inclusion can be slow
Let's keep moving the narrative forward
and give thanks to all who help us grow

Instagram @rebecca_caine

Quotable Quotes

"Too many of us still believe our differences define us."

John Lewis

"Listeners enjoy a huge number of old comedies from the archives, on occasion we edit some episodes so they're suitable for broadcast today, including removing racially offensive language and stereotypes from decades ago, as the vast majority of our audience would expect."

AT WORK

By Rebecca Caine

In a meeting
Feeling quite bored
It's ethical policy
It's mandatory

At a desk
Slide show's on
Taking notes
A 70's video comes on
…And then that word

A discussion
…That word again
Things have changed
That was in context
We weren't woke then

Make edits
It's a classic
Make it suitable
As the 'majority' expects
…Then that word again

...That word
It's ice in my veins
Poison in my gut
I'm at work
I thought I was safe

Session ends
I walk out
I'm ashamed I said nothing
I'm ashamed I froze
I'm angry the chill stayed in my bones

Instagram @rebecca_caine

Quotable Quotes

"No matter who we are or what we look like or what we may believe, it is both possible and, more importantly, it becomes powerful to come together in common purpose and common effort."

Oprah Winfrey

UNAPOLOGETICALLY BLACK!

By Peju Abuchi

I am Unapologetically Black
And that is a fact!
Doesn't mean I lack
Or carry the hashtag #slack
It means a caring community
Has always got my back!

I am Unapologetically Black
And that is a fact!
My hero is Obama, Barack
And not Jacques Chirac
I don't live in a shack
On the contrary, my name is engraved on
the White House plaque

You are Unapologetically Black
And that is a fact!
Doesn't give anyone the right
To devour you like ribs on a rack
Remember, you've developed the foresight
To move forward from hindsight

You are Unapologetically Black
And that is a fact!
This gives YOU the knack
To be authentic and awesome
Anyone looking for brilliance?
In bucket-loads, you got some!

We are Unapologetically Black
And that is a fact!
This isn't about carrying Santa's sack
And handing out gifts
Once a year, in October
As though we cease to exist between
November and September

We are TOGETHER Unapologetically Black
And that is a fact!
Doesn't mean we'll take the flack
For anyone's conniving attack
It means we will act and carefully unpack
Our diversity, dignity and divinity
That will be our lasting impact!

And now to recap and be exact...

Unapologetically Black is
Beautiful and black
There is nothing we **L**ack
Awesomeness is found in our sack
An empowering **C**ommunity has always got our back
We've got a **K**nack for blowing
expectations right out of the ball-park...

I am Unapologetically Black
And that is a fact!

You are Unapologetically Black
And that is a fact!

We are TOGETHER Unapologetically Black
And that is a fact!

The fact is that
WE ARE UNAPOLOGETICALLY BLACK!

LinkedIn - Peju "The Spark" Abuchi
Instagram @powerful.poetic.presence
YouTube - Peju Abuchi

"OTHER"

By Serena Malcolm

When I tick a box, I tick other,
but it doesn't tell the story of my Bajan mother
whose French grandfather
meant children would rather
throw her in a river
than dither
and decide
to which side she belongs.
I tick other
but it doesn't sing the song
of the African drum
that beats proud and strong
on my father's branch of the tree
(except for my Spanish granny
looking down on me,
Waiting for me to speak
her native tongue,
But... which one?).
I tick other
but it hasn't begun to explain the freckles
that frame
my bespectacled gaze
as my Irish eyes are smiling your way,
Or the way my hair turns red
on those long summer days,
Or why my skin is so fair
but my hair is so...
nappy?
I tick other

but I'm not happy there's enough capacity there
to sufficiently bear the truth
of my Wheres,
Of my Whos,
My Forbears;
They're reduced to a 5-letter word,
OTHER,
It's obtuse,
It's absurd
that the scourge of this 5-letter word
beside this 4-sided shape
with its gaping chasm of vague
does not describe
what my progenates primed,
Yet still I hide
in its ease,
And to its safeness concede,
As it quenches my need
to cover all bases,
To honour all races,
To capture the stasis
that this shape means to proffer
between father and mother.
So when I tick a box,
I tick other.

Instagram @serena_malcolm

I AM AN AFRICAN AMERICAN

By Zara Koso-Thomas, age 16 years

The world, the cruel, the unforgiving, the beautiful,
the misleading world has labelled me.
As a what?
An unintelligent, unreliable, lazy three fifths of a human being.
Why am I kicked, punched, pelted, spat on, and yelled at?
I am denied basic rights and face countless acts of discrimination.
Why do I fear leaving my home? Fear walking down the street?
Fear Speaking my mind? Because I am Black.
An African American in the "United" States of America.
In anatomy and emotions, I am no different from those who lack
melanin.
Those with pale skin and bright coloured eyes.
Nevertheless, we are treated as though we do not come from the same
planet.
As if the earth does not provide us with the same air.
If I stop breathing won't I die?
If I fall and injure myself won't I cry?
If my heart stops pumping will I live?
If I don't speak the truth don't I lie?
Are we not the same?
Why does my skin colour cause me so much pain?

Quotable Quotes

"Inclusivity means not 'just we're allowed to be there,' but we are valued. I've always said: smart teams will do amazing things, but truly diverse teams will do impossible things."

Claudia Brind-Woody

SECTION 4:

Winning Poems 2023 – Workplace Category

HER LOCKS UNVEILED

By Zab Birch

In a workplace tale, where struggles abound,
I'll share a story, let its essence resound,
Of Afrocentric hair and features that define,
And microaggressions confronted, a burden assigned.

Once upon a time, in a corporate domain,
A woman named Aisha, her dreams aflame,
With grace in her stride, and pride in her locks,
She ventured forward, equipped with talents and talks.

Beauty she carried, in her radiant crown,
Each curl, a statement, her heritage renowned,
Yet behind admiring glances, a truth concealed,
Microaggressions lurking, in silence they wield.

In meetings, whispers of "unprofessional" sneaked,
As Aisha's curls cascaded, soft and sleek,
But she stood tall, embracing her roots,
Undeterred by judgments, dispelling their disputes.

Power she possessed, in her mind and her might,
Knowledge ablaze, like a beacon in the night,
Yet condescension whispered, "token" they'd say,
Ignoring her worth, diminishing her display.

In her work, she excelled, skills she enjoyed,
Yet assumptions persisted, their biases deployed,
As she shared her insights, their minds astray,
Dismissed and belittled, her expertise in decay.

At work, the battleground, where respect should reside,
But veiled in microaggressions, they sought to deride,
Insensitive comments, disguised as jest,
Undermining her efforts, chipping away at her zest.

History whispered, tales of struggles gone by,
Of racial battles fought, beneath the British eye,
From Windrush's arrival to a nation's divide,
Aisha stood tall, breaking chains with her pride.

Her impact profound, in the face of the storm,
A voice of conviction, with each passing norm,
She rose above biases, determined and strong,
To challenge the status quo, to right the wrong.

With polish and expertise, she paved her own way,
Building bridges of understanding, day by day,
For in unity lies strength, a lesson she'd share,
To break down the barriers, with empathy and care.

So let us rewrite this narrative anew,
Where Afrocentric beauty shines, strong and true,
Where microaggressions wither, their power erased,
And workplaces embrace, a culture diverse and praised.

In this tale of triumph, let's find inspiration,
To dismantle stereotypes, a noble dedication,
For a workplace that's just, where all voices resound,
A harmonious symphony, equity unbound.

Quotable Quotes

"The world has only one border. It is called humanity. The differences between us are small compared to our shared humanity. Put humans first."

Nadia Murad

DISCIPLINARY ACTION?

By Broken Glass

A respite for my mind to take,
To heal, restore and gather.
A class on mindfulness and self-care,
To soothe, nurture, and drench in care.

Disciplinary action? How can it be?
For seeking help, for being me?
For admitting my weakness, my fragility?
For asking for support, for tranquility?

A beautiful seafront under thick fog,
A metaphor for my troubled thoughts.
My mind's crystal waters, murky and clogged,
Need cleansing, purging, and freeing of knots.

A deadline, bills, and a full inbox,
A weight that adds to my mental blocks.
Gaslighted by a team-building retreat,
My soul aches for a genuine connection, a true treat.

Disciplinary action?

No, I need compassion and understanding,
Not judgment, punishment, or reprimanding.
My mental health deserves a commanding,
Of care, love, empathy, and befriending.

Disciplinary action?

No, I need to rest and recharge,
To regain strength and resume the charge.
No, I need support and not a mirage,
To thrive, succeed, and keep my mind at large.

Disciplinary action?

No, I need to break free,
From the stigma that burdens me.
To see my worth, my dignity,
And celebrate my humanity.

Quotable Quotes

"We may have different religions, different languages, different coloured skin, but we all belong to one human race."

Kofi Annan

MONKEY CLIMBING A TREE

By Andrae Davis

"It will never happen to me", I told myself
I'll sail through this teaching job like stealth
Students, target me with racism? Not on your nelly
That happens to others, in the media, on the telly

Then, like the Armada creeping from the fog
I'm under attack, no more than their golliwog
A student's desire to feel superior
Power balance shift, teacher now inferior

Scornful words I find left on my car
A boy spouting hate, carving my scar
I am staring down at this crumpled note
"Monkey", "n*gger", "cotton picker" to quote

Word soon spread of that horrific crime
Sadly, swiftly followed by the next time
Despite rumours sending shockwaves that week
Another seeking notoriety, followed like a sheep

He hands me a picture, that of an ape
I ask him "why?", he has no escape
With no good reason, I can only feel
Targeted a second time, my dignity to steal

As I gaze upon this painful "art"
A primal message, ripping unity apart
Adolescent innocence tainted by the truth
Prejudice lives on, even in tender youth

Surely now, I'd experienced enough
My rugged exterior no longer too tough
Yet, like rolling tides ferocious and fierce
A serpent surfaced again, my heart to pierce

I venture to support a student in need
Refusing instructions, needing to take heed
He runs yelling, attempts to impress his clan
"I'm gonna die…I'm being chased by a black man!"

The negative connotations that phrase holds
Black men are thugs, criminals, hearts stone cold
Painful slurs, penetrating arrows in flight
On my mind during the day, through the night

Leeching language latching on
Did I deserve this misplaced aggression?
Sucking richness and beauty from my soul
Still hoping these youths achieve a life goal

No matter how high I climb society's ladder
There will always be those that see
Not an educated man climbing the ranks
Just, a monkey climbing a tree

SECTION 5:

Winning Poems 2023 – Childhood Category

CRABS IN A CRAB POT

By Linda Downs

The school playground
is an angry sea
of children
I anchor myself
safe, by the prefab
Pigtailed girls jump rope
Boys crouch down
argue over marbles
Through the foaming ocean of white
I spy her
skin the colour
of ripe Conkers
Braided ebony plaits
Pink knitted jumper
a matching skirt
The new girl
tethered to the hem
of the dinner lady
who is wading through
the crowds
looking for someone to buddy up
The new girl pulls herself free
A confident wave
in my direction
She steers herself towards
my hiding place
The world stops
Girls in mid jump
Boys in mid battle

Only she keeps moving
My eyes plead
don't choose me
anyone but me
Too late
heads turn in slow motion
The baying crowd no longer tame
pointing and jeering
as she approaches
shouting "look at the freaks"
Oblivious to their taunts
the new girl takes my hand
a smile to rival
the warmth of the sun
her name is Jamila
she says it means beautiful
but the teachers want to call her Lorraine
They say an English name
will help her fit in
The whole school
a breeding ground for sharks
But Jamila will be safe
on my island

Quotable Quotes

"Until we get equality in education, we won't have an equal society."

Sonia Sotomayor

REGRETTABLE

By Janice Whyne

Reprehensible.
Repugnant.
Ruthless.
Remorseless.

Any of those words would be more fitting than 'regrettable'.
With or without the 'truly'.

How absolutely unthinkable that these 4 syllables sufficiently
serve as a response.
This callous act perpetrated against a child sends more than chills
down my spine.
Viscerally violated by this physical manifestation of a historical
misrepresentation of our beautiful Black bodies.

The stolen innocence of a Beautiful Black Girl.

Another addition to the annals of the evisceration of our dignity.
A strip search of your history will prove this to be true.
But you wouldn't condone that, unlike in the case of Child Q.

The adultification of our children is 'deeply disturbing' and yet
not shocking,
Your choice to see us as you see us has been the lynchpin of your
barbarism for hundreds of years. Keeping your institutions in
place and denying us ours.

Birthed into a world where from our first breath to our last, we
struggle to breathe.

Living at the intersection of multiple forces.
Navigating narratives not written by us.
Up against a world which is never for us.
Yet we continue to show up.

Standing with a Child whose life is forever changed.
Her sense of safety: stripped away.
Her sense of self: dehumanised.
Repercussions ongoing with a ripple effect.
All because of someone's sense of smell.

Pause, and think about that.

How has it really come to this?
Despite my intonation, I'm not really asking.
As those who want to know already know.

Review after review.
Report after report.
Recommendations after recommendations.

The three Rs of our modern civilisation.
Will they ever really make a difference?
I'm not being defeatist; just sharing my view.
As this heinous act demanded a response.
And contrary to official opinion — just so we're clear — to call it
'regrettable' is not a response.

Quotable Quotes

"Diversity requires commitment. Achieving the superior performance diversity can produce needs further action – most notably, a commitment to develop a culture of inclusion. People do not just need to be different, they need to be fully involved and feel their voices are heard."

Alain Dehaze

EXPLODING TEDDY BEARS

By A J Pettigrew

There were so many jokes festering in the playground —
Knock! Knock! Who's there?
Doctor, doctor...
Innocent, harmless, feeble and charmless,
We'd groan in derision and drift back to our games.
But then there were the other jokes, the ones
that injected pain. The ones others found amusing
but I never did. Jokes which
spread as diseases, a comedic plague. They were like
poison mixed in milk and honey, razors
swaddled in blankets, or plastic
explosives swallowed by teddy bears.
My friends couldn't understand why I cried, why I shouted
at them to stop laughing. They didn't
see Ryan, tears coursing like bitter waterfalls
down his dark cheeks. They didn't notice
the news on the telly — the shotguns, the marches,
the people dying every day because of a horrible line
drawn between black and white.
Those kids never knew how much hurt, how much hate
was concealed in those harmless, charmless jokes,
how each one told dug the trench
a little deeper, built the endless
barriers ever higher. They never realised
how every word was a hidden bullet, every punchline
a slaver's whip to the heart.
But every time they grinned and laughed,
white demons dancing in their eyes,
I watched the teddy bears explode.

Quotable Quotes

"In the end, as any successful teacher will tell you, you can only teach the things that you are. If we practice racism then it is racism we teach."

Max Lerner

SECTION 6:

Highly Commended Poems 2023

in alphabetical order by poem title

* denotes under-18s

A BROKEN CHILD

By Jacquie Burgwin-Turner

(Verse 1)
 In the year 1970, my young world was shaken,
Left behind by a mother, a heart forever breaking,
But through it all, a faith in God, unwavering and strong,
A blueprint for resilience, a journey to belong.

Taught to obey, suppress thoughts, seek validation,
Told to blend in, stay behind, a life of hesitation,
Confusion about culture, the colour of my skin,
Emotions overwhelming, a storm brewing within.

(Chorus)
I was a broken child, carrying disgrace,
But within me, a gift, to bring joy to this place,
Tears turned to laughter, uplifting those around,
But behind closed doors, a girl lost, never found.

(Verse 2)
As a mental health professional,
I saw the Windrush pain,
Discrimination and racism, a struggle to sustain,
My parents answered England's call, to rebuild and restore,
But faced hate and prejudice, generations endured more.

Lost like a cloud, drifting aimlessly through life,
Identifying as anything but my true self, the strife,
Bleaching my skin, hoping to escape the hate,
But deep down, I knew, I could be anything, my fate.

(Chorus)
I was a broken child, carrying disgrace,
But within me, a gift, to bring joy to this place,
Tears turned to laughter, uplifting those around,
But behind closed doors, a girl lost, never found.

(Bridge)
At 14, I met my love, a new chapter began,
Embracing a new culture, denying who I am,
Education became my refuge, a world that said "I can,"
But still, a void, a disconnection, a silent exam.

(Verse 3)
Married, children, a life seemingly on track,
But divorce, single parenthood, challenges attacked,
The world crumbled, but determination kept me strong,
A better life for my children, a purpose to belong.

Resilience guided me, climbing the corporate ladder,
But in my mid-30s, depression became a constant chatter,
A silent companion, camouflaged within my days,
Trapped in a cycle, emotions in a disarray.

(Chorus)
I was a broken child, carrying disgrace,
But within me, a gift, to bring joy to this place,
Tears turned to laughter, uplifting those around,
But behind closed doors, a girl lost, never found.

(Verse 4)
But one day, a realisation, I was stronger than this,
Overcoming past obstacles, refusing to dismiss,
With support and faith, a spiritual journey began,
On February 21st, 2014, at 3 am.

Therapy and self-reflection, a path to self-discovery,
A programme empowering others, finding purpose and recovery,
Mastering emotions, becoming the best version of me,
A testament to resilience, the power to be free.

(Chorus)
I was a broken child, carrying disgrace,
But within me, a gift, to bring joy to this place,
Tears turned to laughter, uplifting those around,
But behind closed doors, a girl lost, never found.

(Outro)
Join me on this journey, of resilience and transformation,
Embrace your true self, overcome any limitation,
There are no limits in life, shape your own destiny,
Become the best version of yourself, set your spirit free.

A MOTHER'S PLEA

By Sarah Wood

I implore you white people
Talk to your children about race
About the richness of diversity,
So my child does not have to face...

Twice in one week being told
You are brown like poo,
I hate brown people,
Why does this s**t never get old?

Educate, do the work,
Be an ally, stop the hurt

Please white people talk to your kids.
This may not affect you
But avoidance leads
to ignorance and insults too

Where is he from? Is he adopted?
Can he speak English?
You can't be his Mum, he is a different race,
All said to his face!!

Educate, do the work,
Be an ally, stop the hurt

All said in front of my son,
Bit by bit, damage will be done.

The health visitor calling him a hybrid,
Racism starting only a few days after birth,
Education, allyship - know its worth

Please white people, learn for yourself
The history, the brutality, the contribution,
The beauty.
Then discuss,
The change needs to start with us.
White people.

Educate, do the work
Be an ally, stop the hurt

He is only seven,
How much more before he is grown?
2023, yet still we are here
Two racist insults in a week
What lies ahead is what I fear.

Please white people,
Educate, do the work,
Be an ally, stop my child's hurt
Please, please white people...

ANGRY BLACK WOMAN

By Michelle Brooks

Angry Black Woman
I feel all your pain
Angry Black Woman
Your Tears and Your Shame
Angry Black Woman
You're strong and you're smart,
And Angry Black Woman
Don't lose all your heart.

They think that they know you.
They think you're to blame.
Your boss is a liar
This man holds the frame.
It's evil, it's toxic
It's bitter, empowered
And the game goes on
Hour by hour
Minute by minute
Year by year.
Until you're the "other"
Til all you know is fear.

No promotion
No pay rise
The manipulation is real.
They'll humiliate
They'll scare you
And say you don't feel.

You're not to speak up
Because if you to do.
The "Angry Black Woman" name
For you will be true.
So you grab hold of emotions
And tighten your chest.
All the time doing
What you think is the best.
Angry Black Woman
Can you pass their test?
Angry Black Woman
For you there's no rest.

ASSUMPTIONS

By Farnaz Rais

What do you see?
What do you see when you look at me?
A brown girl done good?
EDI boxes ticked?
Woman? Check.
Brown? Check.
Wears a hijab? Uneasy check.

What do you hear?
What do you hear when you listen to me?
A brown girl got lucky?
EDI boxes ticked?
Strange name? Check.
English accent? Check.
Articulate expression? Perplexed check.

What do you assume?
What do you assume when you contemplate me?
A brown girl aided?
EDI boxes ticked?
Educated? Barely.
Successful? Favoured.
English? Never.

Let me tell you.
Let me tell you what you don't care to know about me.
A brown woman with war wounds who earned her place.
Checked EDI boxes didn't denote equity.

I educate.
I empower.
I lead.

AUSTRALIA FAIR

By Sarah Lock

I want to thank you, Australia Fair
For teaching me how to be black.
You know it's funny, before I got here,
I never referred to myself like that-
I was 'mixed-race' or I was 'light-skinned',
Some called me 'half-caste' that kind of thing-
But, when I arrived to this place, Australia,
I got to grips with this skin that I'm in.

See, every time that I'm at a work-party, and
Australia Fair's had a couple of drinks,
Every Tom, every Harry and Dick…
Likes to tell me exactly what they think;
Like,
"Oh, you'll forgive me for saying- I don't mean to stereotype
But I have noticed, all you with *darker* skin, you're so very much
alike"
Or
"Now, don't get offended, or take this comment as an attack
But, it's in your blood to be aggressive, isn't it? It's a common trait
in all of you blacks."
Or when I meet a client face-to-face
After months of nice chats on the phone;
"Oh really! You could have warned me- about- your dark skin
tone!"
How many white women, Australia Fair-
When settling their crying child,
Are approached on the street by complete and utter strangers

Wearing a smug little smile- with

"Oh Dear! Let me find his mother! How could she leave him with you?!

It's obvious from your appearance, that you've not a clue what to do...

Oh... He's your baby... but he's so pale.... Congratulations!"

I thought you were sorry, Australia Fair

Not still stealing generations.

Recounting these true conversations,

Truly fills me with pain

I get angry, and I get loud, which just serves to vindicate the Fair Australian way-

So instead, let me share some lessons that I've learnt:

Superiority can't be taken

No, it must be earnt.

You want to tell me that you're greater?

Part of the fair majority?

Well let me tell you in return

I am no ethnic minority!

I am one of ninety percent of this planet's population

Who can't be described as fair, or white, or Caucasian

So, before you go asserting that we are down, or we are under-

Check your facts Australia Fair, because- I've got your number!

FIRST DAY

By Olugbemi

"What is your name?"
I sigh, exasperated.

The answer is a shadow obscuring the sun.
I bring heavy thunder clouds
And the room sinks into pandemonium under the torrential rain.
Some people are well-prepared, whipping out their umbrellas
Asking for
Shorter versions
Easier alternations
Reasonable adjustments
And offering suggestions.
Others are bold. The rain hitting them like glass shards
As they tell me what they will call me!
A few skirts under tables.
They will be the ones who just avoid my existence.
Or generally indicate in my direction if they are talking to me.
My given name is sunshine after tragedy, a God-given gift.
Though at their inconvenience, I cave and accept their assortment
of shorter versions
And remind myself that meaning is irrelevant in assimilation.

FOLK TALES AND FABLES

By Laurie O'Garro

It was wrong of me to speak to Miss Right
about what it was like to be me,
Because to her, everything was black and white:
I was black and she was right.

She called all the shots:
If you were right-wing, all white, alt right
you were wrong.
And in her world, that was all right.

But if I said there was more to being right-wing
than swastikas and righteous white knees nestling on necks.
If I used words like *nuanced* and *faux indignation*.
If I exposed the fatal flaw in her……
Right on, white progressive, bitesized Tweets,
Then Miss Right became Snow White,
And I became an angry hag.
And before I could utter another word

Snow White, previously Miss Right,
turned into a princess, and I
turned into a pea,
An insignificant yet clear and present threat
to her fragility.

Not *that* kind of fragility.

No, *hers* had an *exceptional* kind of legitimacy

that set her apart from......
Boys who were proud,
And leagues of defensive gentlemen.

Hers was the fairy tale kind,
Where, with one prick of a malevolent spindle,
She lost consciousness, pleaded innocence,
And pointed a bloody finger in my direction.

Miss Right would have you believe
she's an ally in the 'struggle' for equity,
When really she's biding her time.
Withholding her true identity.

And one starry night, she's absent,
Appearing the next morning, on the arm of Prince Charming.
And you realise she was Cinderella all along and, transformed,
Your struggle is no longer hers.

Miss Right is a shapeshifter,
Moving between black and white worlds,
Fluent in the language of your pain,
But never *really* needing to *feel*.

Because your pain is her gain.

Silently, she asserts her right
to dwell in a world of folk tales and fables,
Where innocence trumps honesty, and
bubbles must never be burst.
Where little black boys and little black girls skip through forests,
Blissfully oblivious to the dangers
beneath that red hiding hood.
Knowing without knowing that

her sweet words are designed to out-fox
their sheep in wolves clothing, because in her world,

Fair is foul and foul is fair.

GET BACK IN YOUR CAGE

By Neleh Yartel

Disguised as a bossy company director,
"Get back in your cage" said the immature white dictator,
To me, to hear,
His team there to jeer,
His antics, being the main instigator.

"Get back in your swamp!" was another comment from the list,
Said to me in a state of insist,
To them, I was different,
Colourful and intelligent,
And from most meetings excluded and dismissed.

In this estate agent, everyone was white,
Colluded with each other for a verbal fight,
Mine was the only black face,
In this all white workplace,
Constantly abusing my human right.

They all thought they were very funny,
Individually, stupid as a dummy,
It is true what they say,
About white racists on display,
"A pea for a brain" forever will they be.

How did this treatment make me feel?
Upset and angry as this was a big deal,
Should I stay or should I go?
To leave would be a huge blow,
So hurt, I needed to heal.

I wish I could have seen that white dictator's face that Monday morning,
When I sent my termination email without warning,
I was finally in control,
Of my determined plan for parole,
Me leaving his appalling estate agent abruptly he wasn't expecting.

It wasn't nice to hear that white dictator beg and plead,
Perhaps he should have taken heed,
Of the damage that had been done,
To my black face and self, the only one,
His hopes of me returning were held on by a single reed.

Two years on, that horrendous episode has affected me deeply,
Shattered my confidence with a deteriorating and fragile mentality,
My trust in future employers has declined,
But I am so glad I resigned,
A long emotional journey I'm on, returning back to my bubbly
personality.

HOW BHM HAS ME FEELING

*By Riley Taylor ***

Over time, I have cultivated a necessary life skill.
Imitation.

Imitation is a foreign concept to most.
Imitation is how I survive.
I can watch, learn, copy, and repeat.
I've done it since the first day, walking through those swinging doors,
When I came to a realisation -
The realisation that I was being watched,
That my skin was being read.

Those looking eyes, judging you?
They're sharp enough to cut you.
{pause}

I watched from the corner the people that were accepted,
Acceptance granted without being second-guessed.
I watched, and I learned.
I applied.
Is everything in place? Is my hair okay enough? Do I appear welcoming enough? Do I seem happy enough? Am I smart enough?
Do. I. Look. Like. You. Enough?

I am not me,
I am a Fraud.
I need to breathe, but the air is thin.

I am in a disconnected trap,
One wrong move, and I lose.
Cracks in my act make themselves known.

Sadness and anger have the ability to blind me as
Easily as getting pushed by in a compact space,
Being collateral damage for someone else's benefit.

I've grown tired of assimilation.
I don't want to be forced to copy and repeat.
I want to go back to the place I never existed in.
Where I don't have to worry about niceties.
Where dancing on clouds is a fathomable experience.
Where my moves aren't being watched.
When I can breathe without restraint.

I go back to fix my appearance,
Not a hair out of place.
Dreaming of a world that doesn't exist.

(BHM = Black History Month)

MEETINGS

By Farnaz Rais

You're all welcome at this meeting, we value your opinions.
A fly in the ointment,
A hair in the soup,
A foot in the jammed door,
A place at the table, sit in a broken chair.
Interrupted
Talked over
Ignored
Deep breath…
Projected voice
Aggressive!
Silence.
Surrounded by the same.
Sitting in my darkness.
You're all welcome at this meeting, we value your opinions.

MRS ABLE

By Dean Gordon

It was 1973 when you were first introduced to me
You looked at me with disdain and said that I was the one to be blamed
A white child named Michael spat in my eye
I was only defending myself in the playground and I was only aged 5
Although Michael spat in my face all you could see was my race
You punished me for kicking but let Michael go
You forced me to wear your plimsolls with a pin in the sole so that blood
in my foot would flow
I screamed in pain you gave me that look again and said don't shout!
You said you would clean up my language then you put soap in my
mouth
Before this I liked school and thought I could trust you
After all you were the Headmistress of C********** Infant School
My screams and tears were nothing to you,
Instead you sent me to an ESN school
You labelled me as educationally sub-normal in 1973
I sometimes wonder how I became a professional with a Masters Degree

(ESN = Educationally sub-normal)

NEVER STOOD A CHANCE (AN ODYSSEY)

By Juley-Ann Smith

Overrepresented in insecure jobs,
Confidence bereft with workplace cultures that cost
a woman like me to lose every trust,
I'm done with working in these spaces with YOU.

I felt high, I'd accomplished a great interview,
Thrilled to be recruited after what I'd gone through.
mobility challenge; physio building my endurance,
have to work lesser hours than once I could do.

W*as* agreed *that I'd work* closer distances to home,
they referred me to their colleague with the schools where I
would go.
Couldn't wait to tell my children *I'll be* bringing home the dough,
and soon we'll have a healthier income cash flow.

My consultant smiled and she shook my hand,
As she welcomed me on board I felt my grin expand.
My heart skipping, I was flying, I felt *high* on my pride,
I'm the sun, I'm a star and I'm shining my light!

My enhanced DBS was checked and passed,
there was nothing more the company needed to ask,
I'd met their every request and they were satisfied
with the safeguarding test I had passed online.

Every document required I had brought had been checked,
they scanned, I was hired, I was ready and set,
Until... *[clap twice]* That Laura event,
Until... *[clap twice]* That Laura event!

Now, Laura was the woman I was told to speak to next.
I happ'ly dialled her number and she answered brightly "Yes?"
I gave my introduction and she uttered with her quip,
"Ah yes, you're the woman with the walking stick".

I let that pass *[clap twice]*
I felt it best... *[clap twice]*
It was just...a harmless little slip,
but what Laura next came out with and I tell you she did switch
to a sharp toned inquisition I felt troubled by this,
"Have you, criminal convictions that the DBS have missed"
Hol' up! *[click twice]*
                              I had to sit.

Criminal convictions? Where's she going with this?
On file; cv, photo and a cleared DBS,
Application, registration form and certificates.
With dyslexia-dyspraxia included with this.
There were things she hid behind her words to leave me speechless
And in my pause *[clap twice]*
She launched her question again.

I Inhaled *and* Exhaled
Felt Ancestor intuition
and the 'them that feel it know it'
you may sense the situation.
And I thought just let me check
as it seemed from my impression,
she'd gone and crossed a line with her out'a order question!

For the record when I called Enquiries DBS,
They told me Enhanced "is the highest - it's as deep as it gets".
In fact, they even told me she'd been so incorrect,
I know this now; I knew back then in retrospect.
Having asked her if she'd checked my file to call her bluff,
she huffed "not *every* check processed
is enhanced enough."

And you know when you KNOW something weird's going on?
can't put your finger on it, you know *she* knows she's wrong.
I was raised to know 'you can't be - wrong *and* strong'.
Spirit told me she and me aren't gonna get along.

I thought about my rent and how deep my arrears,
court summons and unpaid debts stirring up all my fears.
Must take another bullet having got this far,
Forget grey hairs, aging body and old racist scars.

Reaching out to The Creator and my spirit guides!
I ask them "Quell these hot tears rising as they're burning my eyes."
I need this work and she's the one standing at the door,
she's got the keys,
so keep my vision because I've been here before.

Lip bleeding, tongue sore,
mouth dry and splitting,
my jaw tense as I attempt to gain some equal footing.
Bitter-sweet I curtly smart and make it very clear
"I have *no* criminal convictions, n*ot one* spent, *nor* undeclared"

Humiliated and degraded
fingers cramped around the phone,
Laura switches to her 'Shirley Temple',
"I've got to go,
Have to contact one of my covers,
before they leave by four, for home."
Conversation done and Laura hangs up the phone.

Dazed and feeling wounded,
I couldn't put my finger on it.
It was possible that 'Race' had sullied my employment,
It was subtle, there *was something* there, so I went back to my consultant
who giggled, "Oh that's Laura being funny with her weird sense of humour."

Now you and me we know 1 + 1 equals 2
Which is why that *'excuse' simply* will not do.
To try to hide behind the trope that "it's just a joke"
 Undoubtedly now makes you just as much the problem too.

My grievance went along the chain
to the regional director.
And he'd been prepped
So, no surprise it didn't get any better.

Biased with his opinion, kept interrupting what I had to say,
Believe it, he even went as far to reframe
So as not to cast aspersion on Laura's 'good' name,
She his colleague, she his friend of more than a decade

And he claimed she'd been a victim some time ago.
His story goes that Laura's trust had taken a blow
She'd experienced a drama that she never forgot
Where a cover she'd supplied had put her in a spot.

It seems the school in question was her precious alma mater
She felt she'd let them down and was trying that much harder
To ensure the covers that she sent had full identification
even if it meant making her own investigations.

"and what's that got to do with me?" I put to the director
That's what happened in the past I'm new and I've never met
her."
"Well, she deserves from you some sympathy, if you think how
this affects her
 And yes I can see she should not have asked you that question."

"Ah, so you do agree, that was an unfair question!"
"Now you're nit-*picking* everything, from everything I just
mentioned."
And the discussion ended poorly, and no work came my way
And to be honest, words fail me. I don't know what to say.

They closed ranks and she went absent
They said she'd gone on leave,
We know how this always plays out
They simply wait for you to leave.

(DBS = Disclosure and Barring Service; a way for an employer to check if someone has any criminal convictions or cautions)

NOT/IN YOUR FAVOUR

By A K Castellan

Don't do it, don't push it there's
Just no chance.
A kindly hint to stay in my mixed lane.
Lucky to be here at all – and yet
Aren't we all a genetic lottery?

Oppressed and oppressor,
Fully as one.
Harmonised in a juggled blend
Of paradise-blue chained voices,
And stiff upper lips stained red.

Odds stacked on the wrong
Side of white.
I rolled the dice in my favour
And here I stand. Brazen in my
Breathing. Hoping. Living.

I stride and puff through these
Hallowed halls.
Tracing the gilded paths
Of princes and politicians
With steel and steady hands.

Blackness splashed in my name
And my skin.
Ghosts of global violence past

Echo their screams in marble.
Today, I am the nightmare.

A chance on a chance
Brought me here
To the heart of modern empire.
Look close enough and
Every breath is a miracle.

SCHOOL SURVIVOR 1984

By Rabia Begum

Do we all look the same?
In your picture frame?
Brown faces, black eyes,
beholden to racist lies.
Unfulfilled children's rights,
in schools full of whites.
hypocrites of the law,
ignore what you saw.
"Oi you ugly bl**ki",
"go home curry munching p*ki".
But my parents are Indian I protest,
and my skin is definitely blessed.

With crutches in place,
I hobbled to race.
GCSE's, A Levels,
gold stars and medals.
But damaged self-esteem,
crushed the Asian dream.
"You can't be one of us"
for reasons because,
even the bluest eyes,
could not disguise,
the prejudice and hate
that failed to liberate

me.

SELF-RACISM

Alexandra Thomas *

Young little baby, black girl,
Born earlier than expected.
March sun. April breeze.
Then, she didn't know colour nor creed.
Only: to cry, to eat, to sleep.

Young little black girl,
Afro curls kept in unkempt bunches.
Minnie Mouse hair ties embracing all of her textured surface.
Watching people walk by, miniature figures.
To her, the world felt so small and distant.

Blind to difference.
Visible to change.

She's grown up so fast or so they say.

At the tender age of 17.
Praying a trade for the black.
Wishing she was white.
I mean, maybe she wouldn't look so masculine if:
She just painted her skin the purest white,
bleached her hair a golden, sandy blonde
and changed her name to Stacy.

Young little black girl,
Wondering why she fails to love herself.
Don't know how she'll ever love anyone else.

She's just waiting for the day,
When she can believe.
Aphrodite stumbled upon her.
In her sense of being, in every mite of her worth.
Hoping she'll do the young little black girl inside, proud.

CATEGORY: CHILDHOOD

THE DAMAGE YOUR WORDS DO

By Leah Hodgson-Clark *

She looks in the mirror like she does every day,
It's her normal routine.
But this time it's different,
She doesn't see, glowing, melanin skin,
Or beautiful Caribbean curves,

She finally sees what everyone else does.
She sees a weakness, a disadvantage,
She sees a canvas of insecurity,
That our society has created.
That every passing comment, racism or microaggression has created,
She has never seen herself the way she does now.

She's drowned in self-doubt,
This is the moment, she had feared,
This is the moment every black girl has gone through.
This is the moment where all those comments finally got to her.
No matter how much she tried, she couldn't brush it off, not anymore,
Society had finally broken her.

Her sassy, unfazed spirit,
Her magical laughter,
Her unapologetic self was gone.
Now she understood,

She understood the way this world truly sees black beauty:
Aggressive
Ghetto
Dramatic
And dangerous.

She walked past the mirror without even a slight glance,
It was now her normal routine.
She avoided anything that could place her in those stereotypes,
And she hated herself for it.
Instead of seeing her stunning dark skin,
Her irresistible thick curly hair,
And her strong, confident aura,
She saw what your words had made her see.
Instead of what she truly was,
A dark-skinned goddess.

THE INITIATION

By Simon Smailes

He was an impressionable lad,
In every bottom set at school,
Wearing the broken home badge;
Teenage driftwood, bored with life,
Yet blinded by the racists
Into believing their evil words.

Hiding from the neon glare,
His lager-fuelled crew called out,
"Go on, be a man!"
"Do it. Do it! DO IT!"

So he took the knife they offered,
Held it in his hand,
Surveyed it, caressed it,
Felt its threatening menace.
"Do it. Do it! DO IT!"

Adrenaline swept him forward,
Stomach churning, heart pounding,
Watching his drunken prey stumble,
Then fall to the ground.
"Do it. Do it! DO IT!"

The blade cut deep and hard,
Again and again and again,
Through flesh as pink as his own,
Beneath brown teenage skin.

Too late to make amends,
Tears streaming down his face,
He sat alone.
His crew long gone,
No chanting from behind.

Only silence.

THE INNOCENCE OF A CHILD

By Poetry Girl 3.0

As a child, I couldn't comprehend
Why people treated others as less than a friend
Skin colour, language, or culture unique
Why did it matter? What did they seek?

I wanted to play with everyone the same
Laugh, learn, and have fun, it was not a game
But I saw how some were pushed away
Judged, ridiculed, and made to pay

My innocence couldn't understand
Why humans caused such hurt in this land
Their words and actions stained with hate
Creating wounds that would take long to abate

But even as a child, I vowed to be
A friend to all, no matter what I see
To break down the walls and shatter the chains
That racism constructs, causing only pain

For in the end, we all are one
Beneath our skin, we all shine just like the sun
So let's build bridges, not walls, my friends
And, cherish the diversity and the human race to which we belong.

THE WORKPLACE IS FULL OF IT

By Ruby Joseph

I've seen it all, I've seen it all
Racist activities big and small
The workplace is full of it
So now let me open the door
And ask that you give me the floor.

Before you say we complain too much
Sit tight, hold your thoughts and such
The workplace I tell you is full of it
I hope you listen closely to what I say
Because my examples will make your thoughts sway.

Why do you proclaim we're articulate
Whenever we choose to speak up and debate?
The workplace I tell you is full of it
Do you know you reserve that word mainly for Black folks?
What happened to the rest of the working blokes?

Did you dear colleague misjudge our abilities?
If so, then know you offend our sensibilities
The workplace is full of it
That word lets us know your expectations for us are low
So pay attention and realise that we are not slow.

Even though your sense of superiority shines through
You don't seem to know it and that makes me very blue
The workplace I tell you is full of it
You can instruct and lecture me with your door wide open
But when I dare respond back you rush and close it; should I not
have spoken?

Sometimes I don't think you even realise
That your actions bring sadness and our demise
The workplace is full of it
So perhaps you can pause and forget my colour?
Instead, see me and treat me with kindness, fairness and valour.

THEM AND US

By Olugbemi

As a child, my parents told me stories about them –
them and us they said, we are not welcomed here, they insisted.
But naïve and innocent, I did not quite understand what they meant.
I was blind to the chains on my father's feet.
Once a mighty Nigerian doctor, skills in the UK now obsolete,
Driving a bus to make ends meet. Head down, dodging discrimination,
Bringing home bread for his children to eat.
I didn't hear my mother's laments about parenting so far away from
home,
Desperately trying to make this bleak country her own, but instead met
with rejection.
I heard my mother's tongue, but all the words sounded weird and wrong,
Not at all the melody that it should have been.
No. As a child, I saw love and opportunity.
I was excited for all that the big wide world had in store for me.

I didn't see my brown skin as charred until I was told that my A's were
dirty –
My effort negated, because apparently universities held open doors,
diverting destiny
And saving me from being that young black kid, claiming benefits and
popping out babies.
I learned to see my difference from the way the security guard darted
from aisle to aisle, laser focused on me as I bought pick and mix.
I was made to feel disgusted in my skin when older men called me
chocolate
And made comments about my young face and mature body whilst I was
in school uniform.

As I grow older, all I see are labels, divisions, and fear.

My friend's a Muslim, but they call her a terrorist.
Bashing into her as she weeps, whilst people walk past uninterested.
And though her English weaves webs around most, when she speaks
Gujarati,
They sneer at her "speak English please!"

I am told that there is diversity in the student body
But no one can tell me where the black postgraduates and academics
were.
Not even one token black person to meet that quota.
It leaves me reeling seeing this obvious glass ceiling that we are all
ignoring and perpetuating.
They attempt to placate me with their zero tolerance policies –
Yet they ask for a shorter, easier version of my name without even trying
because eight letters cause so much difficulty just like Isabella, Courtney,
Victoria, Dominick, Penelope.

They tell me that they are allies.
I see this every time when they say the n-word then offer a sincere
apology
Whilst insisting that it is only a mere word anyway
I see it too when another POLICE LINE DO NOT CROSS appears in
the estate.
Just another family member stabbed or shot.

See, my parents told me about them and us.
And I dare say that they were right. Quite right indeed.
But I boldly say that they were wrong because there is so much
fragmentation
Because looking within my own black community
There is colourism, islamophobia, antisemitism, homophobia.

Mixed race kids are told they cannot possibly understand with their white privilege.

And we are pushing out our children into the wilderness because they are "different."

There is a them,
A them and an us.
But quite frankly, they are us.
Us who put up borders, conditions, constraints, boundaries on love.
Us who love our own but think that it is okay
To discriminate against people who are not the same.
Really, we could all do with loving with the innocence of a child.

THIS TIME IT'S PERSONAL

By Sandra Howell

Absorbing every book I could get my hands on
reality faded away
opening
doors to different worlds
gateways to different lives

I didn't know
photosynthesising words and stories
was making me
grow
discovering
my likes and dislikes
how
to
communicate
unlock my thoughts and emotions
for
readers
to
vicariously
emote
understand and
enjoy
fictions
I
created

realities
I
lived
Reading for
entertainment and
escape
books were my best friends
therapy
I could disappear
nothing could hurt me
when
I was immersed
in a novel universe
I was
Not
walking to school on my own
racist abuse pelting down
like
short sharp showers
feeling like
thunderstorms
feeling
like hurricanes

they didn't know what they were saying
white people parroted
how do you explain
the adults?
parents
strangers
screaming
shouting
at me

flinching
from me
when I was near
talking
at me
as if
I was a 90-year-old woman who had forgotten her hearing aid

It's not fair I would protest to my mum
every time she was
first
in
last
out
of a queue of
whites
at least
they queued.

CATEGORY: CHILDHOOD

TWO STRONG

By Nalo Solo

Too brown
For your brown eyes
Too fat
To have come from your thick thighs
Too smart
Into it I didn't buy
Too strong
I didn't join the lie
Too free
I spoke my whole mind
Too me
Only one on my side

Two now
I birthed a son
He's bronzed
A child of the sun
Hair coiled
Let it not come undone
Too strong
He knows he's the one
Two free
Living black joy fun
To me
He can always run

WHAT ARE YOU?

By Alisha Fernandes

I find it interesting that I am mixed race in a way that seems to confuse them all. I'm mixed race with more black than white in my veins but it doesn't show on the outside. I'm not being aggressive I just thought you might be interested.

I found it interesting when they said, "There's no need to be aggressive." because I asked a question.

I found it interesting when they said, "Oh my gosh, you look like twins!" because I was stood next to another person of colour.

I found it interesting when they said, "I prefer you with straight hair".

I found it interesting when they said, "Please don't come to work with your hair out, it's a bit unprofessional."

I found it interesting when they said, "I wanted to make something different and wondered if you could give me any recipes for your food?"

I found it interesting when they said, "You're so pale, are you sure you have black in you?" to then saying, "Oh yeah, you act black actually."

I find it interesting when they claim to want to fight for social justice yet conversations about race they say, "It makes me feel uncomfortable".

I find it interesting that as a society we have evolved in many ways, yet racism is still the same.

I find it interesting when they ask, "What are you?".

I find it interesting that it matters.

I find it interesting that it's interesting to them.

I find it interesting that they can choose when I am allowed to fit in and when I am not.

I find it interesting that I am mixed race in a way that seems to confuse them all. There's more black than white in my veins but it doesn't show on the outside. I'm not being aggressive, I just thought you might be interested.

WHAT HAVE YOU LEARNT?

By Annie Alleyne

Part 1: A friend's journey

What do you see when you look at me?
Do you see a child with learning difficulties?
Do you see a child who struggles to retain information?
Or someone so challenging they should spend all their time in detention?

It's true, I'm someone who struggles with learning …
gaining accolades, I'm constantly yearning.
It's true, I'm someone whose brain works differently …
because of an incurable, invisible, disability.

Do you see the challenges I'm faced with?
Like making myself heard and taking in the written word.
Do you see my creativity, my artwork, my debating skills, my bravery?

Do you see me raising my hand, to let you know I don't understand?
I'm confused and yet you look right through me,
When the embarrassment and shame threaten to consume me.

And why is it you don't seem to care, or even notice that I'm there?
Hello … Hello … I'm right here, filled with anger, doubt and fear.
And I'm worried, so worried that I'll never get it,
And that you'll never realise … I'm not stupid, I'm dyslexic!

Part 2: My journey

When I was at school, I wasn't thick,
In fact, I actually thought I was quite sick.
Dissing those who didn't get it,
Like the struggling, challenged, dyslexics.
They didn't get the lessons or the literature,
Me though, I took it in and spat it out like it was scripture.

I was reading before I could walk,
Writing before I could talk,
Then conversing in different languages,
Exam scores waaaaaay above the averages.

But, standing out and being exceptional,
Was scary as hell and emotional.
And standing out became problematic,
For me, a black kid, a minority ethnic.

In a school full of whiteness and privilege,
And me, the only person with dark skin,
Dreading the songs that they used to sing,
Like their favourite … "brown girl in the ring".

But now ... What the hell is happening?
Down go my grades and my reading.
Down goes my confidence in everything.
All of a sudden, I'm shrinking,
Missing school, smoking and drinking.
Finally, starting to feel like I fit in.

Fit into place like a jigsaw, slotting in nicely now with mediocre scores.
And now, I'm no threat to the hierarchy … because now, I'm just
another, average, darkie.

WHEN YOU GROW UP

By Emma Evans

when you grow up
find a nice white man to marry
because this, she says, running her fingers along my arm
this   isn't good

find a nice white man to marry
your children will have it better –
this   isn't good
she says to five-year-old me

your children will have it better –
won't have the problems you're going to have
she says to five-year-old me
i nod at my favourite auntie

it won't be easy for you
because this, she says, running her fingers along my arm
this   is going to make things difficult
when you grow up

WHERE THE MONSTER CRUMBLES

By Jonxthon*

In offices of glass, where shadows roam,
The monster finds a cruel home.
Innocence tainted, dreams unfulfilled,
The heartache of bias, unkindness distilled.

Or in playgrounds, where laughter should reign,
The monster inflicts a deep pain.
In tender hearts, scars quietly grow,
Drowning potential, stifling a great glow.

Yet, let us strive for a brighter day,
Where the monster crumbles, fades away.
Inclusion and love, our guiding light,
A world where all colours shine ever so bright.

WHERE YOU CAME FROM

By Zainab Tasneem

My name isn't amongst the list of those most common
I can never find it engraved on a coffee cup in the office
I can never hear it pronounced the way my mother says it

I lay in bed at night
Wondering if it really matters
If getting my identity right
Really matters
Or that maybe if I
Repeat the way you say my name enough times
It'll be institutionalised in my veins
Until the meaning is no longer in the palm of the hands which
my parents gave
They gave me them to build upon the foundations they've laid

Maybe that'll be easier for you
After all, who wants to endure the hardship of trying to untangle
the tongue's noose
That's not the type of fun you'd want to go through
My ancestors have already tried and tested it
And they're still trying to make it loose
I meant around their mouth
But now you mention it, also their hands
Their body, tight from the shackles of man
They could give up but never have
Their hearts have always soared
Let me explain it more…

You see, they'll happily empty your bins
Sweep the streets they're not welcome in
Drive the vans in the middle of the night
Not kiss their kids goodnight
Just so they can keep them alive
And they'll do all of it with a smile
Go that extra mile
And let's not forget the local shopkeeper
All these people you tell to go back home
Will always be the dreamers
They dream to be able to go home after their shift without having
to work that second job
If you think you can do it too, why don't we swap?
Take the place we rightfully earned
Through all the hard work, maybe it's your turn

But before you make your decision, why don't you take some
time out and have a cup of tea
And to make your life easier, yes you can call me Z.
I hope your tongue can manage the last letter of the alphabet
Because soon there'll be nothing left

But then again, we don't want to waste your time trying to get my
identity right
My name is quite a long and complex name to come by
And you've got bigger fish to fry
Pardon me, no that was my grandparents who did that actually
And what you earn weekly is what they made monthly, if they
were lucky
But no, maybe they should go back to where they came from
Because maybe then you'd be able to replace them

No, no, you're right, we can't forget that some of them are more
qualified than others
The doctors, the engineers, the lawyers
Let's just admit
That they've taken your job and the money that comes with it
They saw an opportunity knocking on the door
And they took it all
You'd be able to conquer that medical role that your neighbour
spent years educating for
After all, you do have GCSEs from school
That would come in handy for that, no?
Let's change the subject, this is getting personal now
5 minutes of talking about this is making your head spin around
Quite a lot to take in
A life like this
Doesn't sound like bliss

You're ready to head home
Have a lie down and turn the TV on
I'll head out with you too
After all, I have a job to do

WHITEWASHED

By Leah Hodgson-Clark

Colours.
Red, green, blue, black and white,
It's something you see.
Everything has its own colour,
You walk past hundreds of different shades of hundreds of different
colours every single day and don't even notice,
But you notice me.

You notice that I have the skin of a black girl,
But it's lighter than "normal",
You notice my coarse, thick curly hair,
You notice that my eyes are dark, my lips are bigger, and my nose is
flatter,
But what you really notice is my skin, and more specifically the colour of
it.

In the summer the melanin glows,
But in the winter, it's a mere tint that barely sparkles.
Black.
White.
Two races that have never seen eye to eye,
Yet somehow I'm a product of them both,
Yet somehow I'm only seen as one.

Black OR white,
Never black AND white.
I can never be white passing for I am too dark,

But I can't know and understand all things that come with being black for
I am too light.
But still I am black enough to face discrimination,
But surely not because one half of me enslaved the other half, right?

I have fairer skin than your idea of a "typical black girl",
I have darker skin than your idea of a "typical white girl".
So that doesn't make sense,
I don't make sense.

I can't forget about my white side,
But always claim your black side.
Don't forget who you are,
But don't forget who you're not.
You're not fully white, you're not fully black,
So who am I?

I AM A MIXED RACE GIRL.
BOTH black and white,
I do have an afro that is curly and thick,
I do have black skin no matter what shade.
I embrace both sides of my culture, never forgetting either of their
history,
I love the diversity that comes with who I am.
I love who I am,
I am a mixed race girl who knows her power and knows her worth,
always.

YOU'RE TRIGGERED

*By Sharon Hood ***

You're triggered.
Go ahead and call me the name.
Words fall from your lips and I'm going insane –
Am I to blame?
Have I been framed?
Is being black a topic from which I should refrain?
With such vigour,
You put me down to self-gratify,
Analyse, critique and insist that I
Ought to be silent, compliant.
Too outspoken, I'm not reliant
To be unbiased, remain quiet
And appease the riot
Which you unveil on my skin:
My colour; my everything.

Black like the cracks in my soul,
Dark like the acts you do which
Prevent me from being whole.
Brown like dried blood on the
Crown I have to bear;
Heavy is the head,
Burdened for the skin I have to wear.
Can't replace;
Take up less space;
Can't become a different race.
This is me:
I can't be

Perfect, blonde and blue-eyed.
I have tried,
I have prayed
That things could change.
This curse I cannot rearrange;
Cannot alter;
Cannot fade;
Cannot decide I want to trade
To be lighter;
To be whiter;
Someone closer to your shade.
This is me:
I can't be
Anything other than black.

Am I playing a card?
Or am I paying regards
To those who came before me?
Am I making a mess?
Am I causing distress?
Triggering you
To open your eyes to an issue
You cannot see?
It's bigger than you and me;
Thick like the blood in our common ancestry.
Yet I call it out and you are outraged:
Deranged to be upstaged
By someone you wish was caged
Just like back in the days
When I was under your control –

My bad, let me stop; I realise
You didn't expect me to rise,
Find a compromise and use your lies
To uplift and propel me to reach new highs.
Within my words, I've given you no place to hide:
The white spotlight shines brightly on you,
Illuminating all that you choose to do
Maybe you don't like my words
Because they're true;
And now
You're triggered.

SECTION 7:

About Black in White

About Us

Black in White is a social enterprise that was established in late 2020 following the publication of an eponymous book of poems that I wrote about some of my experiences of racism in the workplace. I was motivated to write these poems following the murder of George Floyd in May 2020.

Like so many of us, I was deeply struck by how entrenched and endemic racist attitudes continue to result in such horrifying killings and the daily demeaning of Black people. I reflected on my own experiences of racism – particularly while working in the corporate world for nearly 30 years where such things were rarely spoken about – and decided to tell some of my stories.

So Black in White was born. Our mission is to use poetry to contribute to conversations around racism in the workplace and childhood. We seek to open minds with our work and help put an end to racial inequality.

Our Products

To date, Black in White has published four poetry books with poems by over 100 contributing poets and me about racism in the workplace and childhood, resulting from the annual Black in White Poetry Competition. The poems tell stories and share ideas and learnings to help make the corporate space and educational environments more inclusive.

Black in White also produces 4-page discussion guides, A4 posters and A5 postcards designed to help foster important dialogue in teams and for individuals around some of the key themes of equity, diversity and inclusion.

The Black in White books are available for purchase from most major online book retailers, priced from £9.99 to £14.99 + postage & packaging. The books and the rest of our product range can be obtained and from our website: https://www.blackinwhiteservices.co.uk/store/, priced from £3.99 to £14.99 + postage & packaging).

Our Services

We'd love to hear from you if you are looking for a creative and engaging way to have conversations about racism in your workplace or in an educational setting; to access our equity, diversity and inclusion consultancy or mentoring services; or to ask about bespoke projects. The Black in White team is also available for bookings for presentations, panel discussions and poetry readings.

Sponsorship Opportunities

As a social enterprise, we need support to help us develop products, provide services and run our operations. We are therefore looking to provide sponsorship opportunities for companies and individuals to sponsor our annual poetry competition, book launch events and other customisable items. Do get in touch with if you'd like to explore these opportunities with us.

Our Team

The Black in White team comprises several amazing individuals who work with me and play a key role in helping to plan and implement the Black in White activities and initiatives. Meet each team member individually by logging onto our website to read their biographies.

Contact Us

Contact the Black in White team at
info@blackinwhiteservices.co.uk
www.blackinwhiteservices.co.uk

Follow us on Instagram and X (formerly Twitter): @Blackinwhite27
Connect with us on LinkedIn: Black in White Team
Subscribe and like our YouTube channel: Charlotte Shyllon

"Sharing Poems, Opening Minds"